The Angels

Also by DOM ANSCAR VONIER
Published by Assumption Press

The Angels

Dom Anscar Vonier
Abbot of Buckfast

ASSUMPTION PRESS

2013

✠ Nihil Obstat.
Innocentius Apap, S.Th.M., O.P.
Censor Deputatus.

✠ Imprimatur.
Edm. Can. Surmont
Vicarius Generalis.

Westminster
January 3, 1928

The *Nihil Obstat* and *Imprimatur* are official declarations
that a book or pamphlet is free of doctrinal or moral error.
No implication is contained therein that those who have
granted the *Nihil Obstat* and the *Imprimatur* agree
with the content, opinions or statements expressed.

This book was originally published in 1928
by the MacMillan Coompany.

Cover image: *Angels in Adoration*, Benozzo Gozzoli, c. 1460

CONTENTS

The Angels

I

Traditional Angelic Nature

There is in every treatment of Catholic thought, unless it be a rigidly technical treatise, that happy mixture of the certain, the extremely probable, and the moderately probable which constitutes a real philosophy, where conservatism and liberalism are congenially blended. Thus in the pages which follow all the things written down are not matters of faith, nor would it be possible in a small volume of this kind to affix a proper theological note to every proposition, distinguishing what is strictly of faith from the conclusions and happy inspirations of minds fond of the things of God; but much edification and instruction can be derived from the sayings of theologians and preachers which are not de fide (of the faith), but rather the legitimate speculations of minds habitually attuned to revealed truth.

Our first authority on the history of the angels, their lives and their natures, is found in Holy Scripture. There is a great oneness in the presentment of angelic character in the various books of the Bible, from Genesis to Apocalypse; the angelic type never alters, we may even venture to say that it never develops as the divine revelation in other matters goes on and gains momentum from century to century; what the angels do at Bethel they do also in the days of Christ, they "ascend and descend upon the Son of man" (John 1:51). Cherubim with "a flaming sword, turning every way, to keep the way of the tree of life" (Gen 3:24) are visions as formidable as any angelophany in Ezechiel or the Apocalypse.

There is not, therefore, in our angelology that progressive revelation of a mystery which is the characteristic of our Christology; the mystery of the God-Man is revealed gradually to the minds of men; not so that of the angels; they are made completely manifest from the very beginning, and though, in the course of the centuries of the faith, angels show forth now one kind of activity now another, their essential behavior is always the same.

The fact is that our Scriptures never teach us anything about the spirits of the invisible world *ex professo* (expressly), they never narrate anything about them as a revelation of their mysterious existence; the inspired writers take them for granted and mention them only in connection with human history, the history of the people of God, and the history of Christ. Nothing is more casual and unexpected than the mention of angels in every portion of the Scriptures; you never know when to expect an angel; there is no set of events of which you could predict with certainty that they would bring an angel from heaven to earth. The same thing which at one moment is done through angelic ministry, at another time is left in its natural setting.

Our Scriptures, then, may be said to accept the angelic world as a complete, self-sufficient, unaccountable power, which cannot itself be altered by the course of human events, but which may influence them whenever it pleases. Nor do the Scriptures distinguish clearly at all times between angelic intervention and divine intervention; the heavenly visitant who is called "angel" passes at once into a role which is obviously divine. This is very remarkable in the oldest angelophany in the Bible—the angel whom we might call the angel of the family of Abraham; the heavenly messenger who spoke to Hagar, the slave-wife of Abraham, is at the same time angel and Lord of life:

> And the angel of the Lord having found her (Hagar), by a fountain of water in the wilderness, which is in the way to Sur in the desert, He said to her: Hagar, handmaid of Sarai, whence comest thou? And whither goest thou? And she answered: I flee from the face of Sarai, my mistress. And the angel of the Lord said to her: Return to thy mistress, and humble thyself under her hand. And again he said: I will multiply thy seed exceedingly, and it shall not be numbered for multitude (Gen 16:7-10).

The clearest instance in Genesis of angelic, as distinct from divine manifestation is perhaps the vision of Jacob:

> And he saw in his sleep a ladder standing upon the earth, and the top thereof touching heaven: the angels also of God

ascending and descending by it; And the Lord, leaning upon
the ladder, saying to him: I am the Lord God of Abraham
thy father, and the God of Isaac. The land, wherein thou
sleepest, I will give to thee and to thy seed (Gen 28:12-13).

There is no mention of angels in the great period before the flood, nor are they described as ministering to
Noah in his peril; the angelic ministry, as a ministry, be-
gins with the history of the Jewish people. In the narrative
of creation there is not the remotest mention of them, and
that the evil spirit should be spoken of long before any
other power of the unseen world shows clearly that the
inspired writers never gave themselves any other task than
the history of man and his vicissitudes. Spirits are not the
theme of the Bible.

One might not unaptly compare the attitude of our
Scriptures towards the spirits with their attitude towards
those portions of the human race which are neither the
Jewish nation itself nor the Christian Church. The peoples who are not the chosen race come frequently into
contact with it, and are even meant to help the people of
God in many ways; the scriptural allusions to them are
therefore very valuable from the historical point of view,
and we learn a good deal about the non-Jewish peoples
from the Bible, though that book is in no sense a history
of mankind at large.

In a similar way the inspired historians and writers,
whilst dealing with man's supernatural career on earth,
have revealed to us much of the unseen world, but only
incidentally, and in so far as it concerns man's eternal wel-

fare. We must bear in mind this relative position of our angelology in the Scriptures, and not expect more than fragments of angelic history; yet those fragments are precious and instructive in the extreme.

It would not serve the purpose of this book to quote and explain all the various scriptural allusions to the spirits; every reader can perform this task for himself. Broadly speaking, we may divide the references of Holy Writ to the angels into four classes—the historical, the liturgical, the theological, and the prophetic.

By historical angelophany I mean all those assertions found in the Bible that spirits did a work, bore a message, or lent their help to humanity from the time of Hagar to that of Peter in his prison. These activities are narrated as ordinary historical events, and they are never concerned with angels in their multitudes, but only with them as individual spirits.

Then there are the liturgical allusions to angelic presence in divine worship; the psalms abound in them, and the "sweet singer of Israel" professes to utter God's praises in the presence of the angels. The "multitude of the heavenly army praising God" (Luke 2:13) at Christ's nativity may be considered under this heading.

As theological references those passages of the Scriptures may be quoted where the heavenly spirits are mentioned, not in connection with worship or missions, but as a portion of the supernatural world; as when Christ is said by St. Paul to be raised up "on God's right hand in heavenly places above all principality and power and virtue and dominion" (Eph 1:20-21), when the same Apostle says that the Christian man has "come to Mount Zion and to the city of the living God, the heavenly Jerusalem, and to the company of many thousands of angels" (Heb 12:22), or when Christ himself says that he will confess the name of his faithful witness before the angels of God" (Rev 3:5), or that there is "joy before the angels of God upon one sinner doing penance" (Luke 5:10). The office of the guardian angels may also be considered as belonging to the theological aspect of angelology; the Scriptures reveal to us a side of the spiritual world which is more than a transient mission, in our Lord's words: "I say to you that their angels in heaven always see the face of my Father who is in heaven" (Matt 18:10).

The prophetic allusions are numerous in the Apocalypse where angels are described as doing great things in the mysterious future; but we have also some such prophetic references in the Gospels themselves, as, for instance, where Christ says that he will "send his angels and gather together his elect from the four winds, from the uttermost part of the earth to the uttermost part of heaven" (Mark 13:27).

If we take the trouble to make for ourselves a complete collection of all the angelophanies of our Scriptures we shall easily gain an impression which might be called the traditional Christian sense concerning the angels. Their character, as I have already said, is clearly marked from the beginning and does not change; their readiness to do God's bidding is as great as their power to perform it; nothing can resist their will, and they never fail; they are always spoken of as being God's own, and at no time is there any fear as to their future.

They carry out the commands of God with unflinching firmness when they are sent forth as the ministers of God's justice, and nothing diverts them from the course of apparent severity. They are standing in the fierceness of God's countenance, and yet the lowliest things of this earth are the objects of their attention, as when Raphael goes to the city of the Medes and finds Gabelus, giving him the note of hand and receiving from him all the money which was owed to Tobias (Tob 19).

The angels are never described as struggling with evil; it is always overcome by the sheer might of their presence. From the Scriptural account of them we learn that they know neither temptation nor suffering. As we study them we are transplanted into a world entirely different from our own—a world where spiritual wealth is the rule, and where moral or mental destitution is unknown.

It could not be said that through all the angelophanies of the Bible we learn anything personal about any one of the angels. There is certainly a variety of those spiritual personages in our Scriptures—some are more important than others, some fulfill missions which are not entrusted to others—but it could not be said that we learn much about these heavenly actors in the drama of the world, as we learn to love, to admire, to compassionate the human actors, like Moses or Elijah or Paul, or, above all, like Christ himself. The angel who comes nearest to human sentiment is the angel who comforted Christ in his agony in the Garden:

> And there appeared to him an angel from heaven, strength-
> ening him. And being in an agony, he prayed the longer
> (Luke 22:43).

But even in this instance how divinely anonymous the heavenly comforter has remained. All this confirms the truth of a remark already made, that the angels are not the princi-pal theme of our Scriptures, but only an incidental one.

There is another most authentic source of informa-tion concerning angelic life, angelic power, and angelic character—the Church's worship, both in its sacramental and in its liturgical aspect. But there also we shall find the same features for which the Scriptures have prepared us, of spiritual aloofness on the one hand, and spiritual help-fulness on the other. The Church considers the spirits as her fellow-workers in the sanctification of the world, and her fellow-worshippers in the adoration of Christ.

The Church's faith in the guardian angels is to be ranked differently; this is not so much an act of the Church as a dispensation of the Creator himself. What I mean here is this, that besides that universal guardianship of man by the angels—of which we shall speak later on—the Church makes use of the angels most freely in her sacramental and liturgical life. In her power of sanctifying visible things the Church seems to know no limit; she calls upon God to send the heavenly spirits and cause them to dwell in the place which she has blessed, to bid them guard the object she has sanctified, to make good the promise she herself has given of protection from the evil one.

The *Rituale Romanum* (Roman Rite) is most instructive from this point of view. The great blessings of the Church, which are, after all, merely an extension of her sacramental power, are extremely bold in their use of angelic intervention. If the Church blesses a bridge over a river, she confidently expects that an angel will be deputed to the keeping of that bridge. The Church prays God to join his angel to the chariot on which her blessing has been bestowed. The angels are called down into the house of the sick, into the home of the newlywed, into the rooms where Christ's little ones are being taught their faith and their letters. There seems to be no end to those angelic possibilities in the sense of the Catholic Church. Everywhere the evil spirits are driven away, and the good spirits are made to take their place.

In the Liturgy, properly so called, the angels play a great role. They are present at the Eucharistic Sacrifice; one of the most mysterious and sacred prayers of the Canon of the Mass introduces an angel who has remained without a name throughout all the centuries during which the prayer has been recited:

> We most humbly beseech thee, Almighty God, to command that these things be borne by the hands of thy holy angel to thine altar on high, in the sight of thy divine Majesty, that so many of us as at this altar shall partake of and receive the most holy body and blood of thy Son may be filled with every heavenly blessing and grace.

At the beginning of Mass, Michael is among those holy ones to whom we confess our sins. When incense is burned over the offerings on the altar the intercession of Michael, "who standeth on the right side of the altar of incense," gives an additional aroma of sweetness to the burning perfumes. Then we have the glorious communion with the angels at every one of the Prefaces of the liturgical year:

> Through whom the angels praise thy Majesty, the dominions worship it, the powers are in awe. The heavens and the heavenly hosts, and the blessed seraphim join together in celebrating their joy. With these we pray thee join our own voices also, while we say with lowly praise: Holy, holy, holy, Lord God of Hosts.

Many other such evidences of the Church's faith in the presence of heavenly spirits round the Christian altar might be quoted from the Liturgies of the East and West. They are for us a very sure guidance as to the nature of our participation in the comity of the invisible nations of spirits. We are as sure of their cooperation, of their love for us, of their knowledge of us, as we are ignorant of the details of that mysterious intercourse. It may certainly be said that the kind of spirituality which the Scriptures and the Church have made their own is a most healthy and most serene contribution to man's spiritual inheritance.

II

History of the Angelic Cult

If the spiritual character of the angels is well defined and clearly marked in our Scriptures, the same thing could not be said of the way in which these mysterious beings are described for man's apprehension. There is no uniform way in the Bible of representing the angels. The most elaborate descriptions, such as the vision of the Seraphs by Isaiah and the vision of the angel by Daniel, are completely baffling to the art of the painter. It is extremely difficult for us to visualize the scenes described so carefully by the prophets, as we are entirely without experience in such matters. The angels of the Resurrection and the Ascension are the most human presentments of the heavenly messengers:

> And entering into the sepulcher, they saw a young man clothed with a white robe (Mark 16:5).

> And while they were beholding him going up to heaven, behold two men stood by them in white garments (Acts 1:10).

The first point of interest, then, in the cult with which Christians have honored the angels is precisely this attempt to make visible the unseen by giving a bodily form to the heavenly spirits. The earliest Christian representations of angels are concerned with the historic appearances, with those spirits who have fulfilled missions in the New Testament under definite names. Up to the fifth century no other angels are found represented in Christian art; and these are given the ordinary human form, with their names in such proximity that there can be no mistake about their identity, just as in the case of the apostles and martyrs. About the fifth century we begin to find mosaics, paintings, engravings of angels generally, without a clear historic reference, and the distinctive symbolic sign becomes prevalent, the wings attached to the bodily frame.

There is quite a chapter of religious development implied in this progressive adoption of wings for the heavenly spirits by the Christian artists of the earlier centuries of our era. We have in Isaiah the first mention of wings in connection with spirits:

> In the year that King Uzziah died, I saw the Lord sitting upon a throne high and elevated: and his train filled the temple. Upon it stood the seraphims: the one had six wings, and the other had six wings: with two they covered his face, and with two they covered his feet, and with two they flew (Isa 6:1-2).

There is no clear evidence that the universal custom which has prevailed from Byzantine times of representing the angels with wings owes its origin to the vision of

Isaiah. The Seraphim as described by the great seer are one of the most difficult subjects to be materialized in art. The two-winged angels are a spontaneous creation of the Christian imagination which in this matter has followed the artistic tradition and intuition of the Western civilizations of earlier times. Nothing is more common in Greek and Roman art of the best periods than to give a pair of wings to a superhuman being. The divinity called Victory is invariably endowed with a glorious pair of wings, and so are innumerable genii. That Christian artists, of all shades of talent, should have pictured superhuman beings in the same way as that in which the pagans depicted them is no more astonishing than the circumstance of a hymn to Zeus being sung in melodies which are adapted to a Christian hymn, or of meters of pagan poetry being adopted by Catholic hymnologists.

There are two instances of the classical art which have passed into the service of the angel worship which are especially striking. Genii or demigods are seen on ancient friezes and sarcophagi carrying the privileged ones of the human race to the ethereal spheres, and also weighing the souls of men in the scales of justice. In Christian art these two conceptions are commonplaces. Angels carry the elect to heaven, and angels weigh the souls of men in the final balances. The period of history when paganism was giving way finally to Christianity under the first Christian emperors is particularly interesting from this point of view. The Victory statues are often adorned with Christian symbols such as the Labarum, and genuine heathen medallions of Mercury have an entirely different signification when the word "Michael" is engraved upon them. Perhaps the owner of the art-reasure was loth to part with his gem, and had a Hermes Christianized into an archangel! (See *Dictionnaire d'Archéologie Chrétienne*, "Anges.")

From the sixth century onwards the angelic type is fixed. With the exception of the Seraphim of Isaiah, who have always been the despair of draughtsmen, angels are given asexual lineaments of body and their garments flow in dignified folds. The alternative forms of winged heads are expressions of beauty which is neither masculine nor feminine.

It was reserved to the latest renaissances, the baroque and the rococo, to lower the majestic type of the best periods of Christian art. Can the name of "angel" still be given to that host of nude figures in plaster or marble which people the continental churches from one end of Europe to the other? It would be difficult to find any principle or justification underlying such handiwork on the part of Catholic craftsmen. The one reassuring thing about those periods of artistic extravagances is this, that at the very time when the artistic representation of the spiritual being was at its lowest, the theological schools of the Church produced some of the profoundest speculations on the nature and the might of the angels.

From the very nature of the case, acquaintance with the angelic world has not progressed as angelic art has progressed. We know of no more angels today than were known in the first century. Michael, Gabriel, and Raphael are the only authentic angelic names. In the first centuries there is often mentioned another angel, Uriel, even by the orthodox. He is invoked in some of the ancient litanies; he is supposed to be the spirit who stood at the gate of the lost Eden, with the fiery sword. But the trilogy of Michael, Gabriel, and Raphael stands nowadays without any competitors.

Superstition there has been in the cult of the angels. In the old Egyptian fashion an angel was supposed to be the Keeper of the Tomb, and to make it inviolable. The Gnostics had their own angelic mysteries. To know the true names of the "Seven who stand before God" was a talisman. St. Paul alludes to the perversion of a great truth which had already begun:

> Let no man seduce you, willing [I.e., by affecting humility and religion towards angels] in humility, and religion of angels, walking in the things which he hath not seen, in vain puffed up by the sense of his flesh (Col 2:18-19).

The intellectual development of the angelic cult in the Church has far exceeded the liturgical and the artistic developments. If art has been once or twice on the point of making the angels vulgar, of turning them into pixies, theology, mystical and speculative, has more than compensated for such a lapse. Angels have become for the Christian thinker a sort of minor infinitude, with endless powers of mind and will.

The great classic of angelology is a work whose probable date is the second half of the fifth century, called the *Heavenly Hierarchy*. It is a portion of the work of an unknown writer who goes by the name of Dionysius the Areopagite. In this book the writer takes for granted that classification of the spirits into nine choirs, and again into three triads within those nine choirs, of which much will be said in the following pages. Quite an original contribution of the author seems to be the doctrine of hierarchic illumination, of which there is no clear trace in the Scriptures. It is, however, a most happy and genial application to a special case of the well-established theological principle of the interdependence of creatures, and the oneness of the created universe.

The angelic manifestations narrated in the Scriptures are part of the traditional Christian Faith and belong to the most authentic history of the people of God. The question now arises whether such angelic manifestations belong to the normal life of the Christian Church in her mighty course through the centuries. It is evident that whatever angelophanies there may have been since the last book of the Scriptures was written, such manifestations are to be considered merely as historical facts, not as things integral in any way to the *depositum fidei*, "deposit of the faith." It is, of course, a matter of faith that the heavenly spirits are associated in one way or another with the life of Christians here on earth, as will be explained by and by in this book. The question now asked is about miraculous angelophanies, such as Peter was granted when he was delivered from his prison; are there on record clear and undoubted interventions of heavenly spirits, under easily observable circumstances in the history of the Church?

There is certainly an a priori assumption in favor of such manifestations; it may even be said that they belong to the ordinary *charismata*, "charisms," of the Church. Spiritual phenomena that occurred in the primitive Church are characteristic of the normal life of the Church, as the primitive Church is the ideal Church.

It has been found as feasible, therefore, to write the history of angelic intervention as to write the history of martyrdoms and missionary expeditions. This task has been carried out with great care and perfect soberness of method by those princes of Christian hagiography, the Bollandists. In their *Acta Sanctorum*, "Acts of the Saints," under the date of September 29, the feast of St. Michael the Archangel, they give an exhaustive survey of all the known angelophanies in Church history. The learned historians deal with age after age from the second century onwards, under titles such as this: *Beneficia Angelorum saeculo quarto*, "The Benefactions of the Angels in the Fourth Century." Thus nothing is easier than to gain from the complete and critical studies of the Bollandists a general impression of the miraculous interventions with which the Christian people have been favored in their long history.

The interventions of St. Michael are considered apart in the *Acta Sanctorum*, and they differ slightly in character from the usual angelophanies of the Catholic Church. More than once, though not as often as might be imagined, Michael, the leader of the celestial hosts, helps the Christian warriors on the battlefield to gain a victory over adverse powers. Moreover, St. Michael has two great shrines in Western Europe towards which kings and peoples have pilgrimed as they pilgrimed to the tombs of the Apostles. Mount Gargano, in Southern Italy, and Mount St. Michel, in Northern France, have been true angelic shrines from the early middle ages; there the heavenly prince has been believed to distribute favors and receive the pilgrim with all the graciousness of a mighty lord.

If we examine now the other angelophanies, century by century, we are struck by their sobriety and their manifest humanness. Rarely, if ever, do we come across anything in history that is of a terrifying nature in angelic manifestations, nor do we find the angels taking part ostensibly in the great struggles of the Christian people. Even the Crusades, which would have been such a perfect setting for the scintillating intervention of heavenly hosts, are remarkably devoid of such glorious legends. Now and then a straggling battalion of Crusaders, athirst and discouraged, is led out from a hopeless wilderness by a mysterious stranger who disappears when the danger is past, but on the whole the angelic ministries, as narrated in Church history, are of a much more private, nay, intimate character.

Angels come and console the martyrs in their prisons, and even heal their wounds, like so many good Samaritans; angels are seen taking care of the bodies of the Christian athletes, which the persecutor had thrown out to ignominious neglect; angels feed the hermits, and manifest to the early monastic lawgivers what is wise and what is excessive in Christian asceticism; they help the solitary to overcome his terrors at the sight of solitudes filled with evil presences; they give warnings of the approaching death of some lonely servant of God, and they are seen carrying to heaven the soul of many a saint.

Quite early in ecclesiastical history we find the angels intimately associated with the Eucharistic mystery. They visibly assist at the sacrifice of Mass, they carry the sacramental Body of Christ to the solitary Christian who would otherwise have been deprived of that heavenly Food; and—what is more striking still—in the very heart of Catholicism, in a well-peopled nunnery for instance, an angel is seen taking Holy Communion to a privileged soul as a mark of special favor. St. Isidore, the ploughman, is helped in his humble work by angelic fellow-laborers; and an angel girds the loins of St. Thomas Aquinas with the mysterious *cingulum*, "girdle" of perfect chastity—a very remarkable attention in the life of the great doctor and thinker, for we do not read of heavenly intelligences whispering to him the secrets of Catholic theology. In the case of Thomas, the angelic ministry is of a much more intimate and personal nature. St. Francesca is favored with an almost constant vision of an angel, whose attention to his protégée is most minute in matters both spiritual and temporal. St. Teresa sees angels carrying, as in triumph, the virginal body of one of her dead nuns; and St. Stanislaus Kostka, detained in the house of a heretic in Vienna, receives the sacred Viaticum at the hand of an angel. An angel brings a lump of sugar to the infirmarian of St. Philip Neri, thus making it possible for the saint to be given the medicine of which he was so sorely in need. Angels are heard alternating with monks in divine psalmody in many a medieval abbey, when the brethren were in need of encouragement during the painful vigil of a cold winter night.

Such are the characteristic angelophanies we find in Church history. There is a sweet sameness about them in all times. May we not say that angels break through the veil of mystery and manifest themselves, not in order to frighten Christians and overawe them, but to smile at them with the smile of love and compassion?

III

Our Scriptures are remarkably reticent as to the nature, the life, and the activities of those wonderful beings whom we call the angels. They show themselves to perform definite missions, to deliver messages, and they disappear as suddenly as they have come. The only trait which the Scriptures seem to distinguish clearly is precisely this agility of motion, this freedom from the trammels of space, and this also, no doubt, is the characteristic in angelic nature which is most attractive to the human imagination. Yet it would be an uncatholic thing to say that we are quite ignorant concerning the nature of the angels. Catholic theology has its own resources, and with regard to angelic existences it has arrived at certain conclusions, which in their outlines may be taken as expressing truth.

Christian thought is not satisfied with the merely ministerial role of the heavenly spirits; the angels are more than ministers and messengers, they are, above all, a portion of the universe, they are its noblest portion; and very early in the history of Christian thought we find the angels occupying a most important cosmic position. There is stability of power and life in the spirit world, and the angels are become great beings on whom the cosmos reposes as on solid foundations. This view is certainly adumbrated in the writings of St. Paul when he speaks of Christ as being raised:

> Above all principality, and power, and virtue, and dominion, and every name that is named, not only in this world, but also in that which is to come (Eph 1:21).

Our theology starts with the principle that angels are pure spirits, and whatever may be deduced from such a principle we may hold as being true. Perhaps we cannot go very far, yet when we find the best theologians writing voluminously on the subject of the angels we ought to admit that much can be said without extravagance of speculation. Some extravagance there may have been at times, as it may intrude into philosophy of every kind, but such excess nowise detracts from the merit of the labors of a sober genius like St. Thomas Aquinas, to quote only one of the great and humble theorizers about the angels.

There is a conflict between Catholic art and Catholic theology in this matter. Catholic art gives bodily substance to the angels; it gives them physical color, visible beauty; whilst it is the effort of Catholic theology to discard every element of materiality and visibility. We need only be reasonable in order to find peace in a contest that cannot be avoided. As we are now, in our mortal state, we cannot think in purely spiritual elements, we must have the aid of our fantasy, and the richest imagination will be the one to conjure up the most gratifying visions of heavenly messengers. But we ought to know that the reality is very different, incomparably different indeed, and immensely more beautiful; we ought not to feel sad if we are told that our visions of angels, if we have such, do not represent the heavenly visitant in his native existence, but that he appears to us in the borrowed garb of imaginative impressions.

What, then, are the certain conclusions to be drawn from the principle that angels are spirits? The following statements may be taken as being widely accepted theorems concerning angelic existence:

1. Angels have a beginning, but they cannot perish; they remain everlastingly the same.
2. Angels are not subject to the laws of time, but have a duration measure of their own.
3. Angels are completely superior to space, so that they could never be subject to its laws.
4. Angelic power on the material world is exerted directly through the will.
5. Angelic life has two faculties only, intellect and will.
6. In the sphere of nature an angel cannot err, either in intellect or will.

7. An angel never goes back on a decision once taken.
8. The angelic mind starts with fullness of knowledge, and it is not, like the human mind, subject to gradual development.
9. An angel may directly influence another created intellect, but he cannot act directly on another created will.
10. Angels have free will; they are capable of love and hatred.
11. Angels know material things and individual things.
12. Angels do not know the future; they do not know the secret thoughts of other rational creatures; they do not know the mysteries of grace, unless such things be revealed freely, either by God or by the other rational creatures.

These theorems have reference to the natural state of the angel. But the angel has been elevated to the supernatural state, the state of grace, and concerning that state some other principles have currency amongst theologians; we must defer them to the subsequent chapter on Spirit Sanctity.

I think the enunciation of the aforesaid theorems is quite clear. Every one of my readers will understand what is meant by the phrases, though he may find it difficult to adjust such ideas to his ordinary way of thinking. The theorems here stated practically cover the whole field of theology; anything beyond this becomes subtlety.

From our Scriptures we know that amongst the angels there is a hierarchy—there are the greater, perhaps the immensely greater angels, and the lesser angels; but it would be temerarious, not to say foolish, to attempt an explanation of those differentiations in spiritual substances. Why is one spirit greater than another? To this we can give no answer. We may say, of course, that a spirit is greater because his intellect is more powerful, because he grasps things in a more simple and limpid fashion, because he sees with one act of mind what other spirits of a lower order can only perceive by many acts; but it is evident that this would not give the root of his greatness. The reason why he can thus comprehend and visualize is because his is a greater mind. Why is his mind greater? Because his is a greater nature. But how is his a greater nature? To this query there is no reply among the children of men. So our theology of the angels concerns itself with the general angelic features, not with their special attributes, and we know no more about the highest angel than about the lowest; we give them the generic attributes which belong to all finite spiritual substances, the human soul alone excepted.

We may now say a few words in explanation of each one of the above theorems.

1. *Angels have a beginning, but they cannot perish; they remain everlastingly the same.*

Spirits, like matter, were created by God's omnipotence out of nothingness; they are no more a portion of the divine Substance than is a stone or a tree, but they resemble the divine Substance in a fashion that is immensely closer, so that by comparison they might be called divine, as God's likeness is in them in a manner in which it is not in other portions of his creation. We cannot say whether all the spirits that now exist were created at one and the same moment, or whether there were different creations. But no finite spirit could create another, and it is more in keeping with Catholic thought to say that God created all the angels together. The distance that separates the present moment from the creation of the spirit world is, of course, not calculable by time standards. Spiritual substance once produced by God cannot decay, it may do wrong in mind and will, but it always remains a perfect substance; it does not change in its essentials, it does not deteriorate in its nature. We could hardly say that it is immortal, because the word immortality would not do justice to such permanence; a spirit is simply unalterable, his changes are merely changes of thought and will.

2. *Angels are not subject to the laws of time, but have a duration measure of their own.*

This has been most beautifully expressed by Cardinal Newman in his Dream of Gerontius, and though the passage is often quoted it would be a neglect on my part to omit it here:

> For spirits and men by different standards mete
> The less and greater in the flow of time.
> By sun and moon, primeval ordinances—
> By stars which rise and set harmoniously—
> By the recurring seasons, and the swing,

This way and that, of the suspended rod
Precise and punctual, men divide the hours,
Equal, continuous, for their common use.
Not so with us in th' immaterial world;
But intervals in their succession
Are measured by the living thought alone,
And grow or wane with its intensity.
And time is not a common property;
But what is long is short, and swift is slow,
And near is distant, as received and grasped
By this mind and by that, and every one
Is standard of his own chronology.
And memory lacks its natural resting-points
Of years, and centuries, and periods.

Newman put into matchless language the technicalities of scholastic theology. Though angels remain for ever, we do not say that they are eternal. Eternity is the measure of God's existence; it implies negation, not only of an end but also of a beginning; it implies, moreover, immutability of every kind, even immutability in intellect and will: such immutability or eternity is possessed by God alone.

3. *Angels are completely superior to space, so that they could never be subject to its laws.*

Our reason assents to this theorem more readily than does our imagination. Reason tells us that a spirit, through the very definition of his nature, has nothing spatial in his composition. Movement, in the bodily, the mechanical, sense of the word cannot be predicated of spirits. They act, they exert power on material things, now at one point of the universe, now at another; these acts or influences are successive, not simultaneous, but it could not be said that a spirit has moved or flown from one spot to another, he has merely exerted two different acts of power over objects that are mutually remote.

4. *Angelic power on the material world is exerted directly through the will.*

Angelic will-power is not only immanent, it is executive; it can alter the things of the material universe by a direct contact or influence. Spirits can work signs and prodigies by making use of the powers of nature, though it could not be said that they can work miracles, in the proper sense of the word, such as the raising of the dead; this would require divine power. Angelophanies, or apparitions of angels or spirits generally, may be explained through the power these lofty beings possess of acting on our sense-perceptions, and of giving us those mighty impressions of which we find instances in the Scriptures:

> His body was like the chrysolite, and his face as the appearance of lightning, and his eyes as a burning lamp: and his arms and all downward even to the feet, like in appearance to glittering brass: and the voice of his word like the voice of a multitude (Dan 10:6).

5. *Angelic life has two faculties only, intellect and will.*

With this theorem we banish from spirit-life every vestige of sense-life. Angels cannot be said to have imagination, passion, sentiment, all of which manifestations of life are essentially the modifications of organic life and sense-powers. This is what we mean by the very common expression "angelic purity." Angels are pure from all sensuality, not through virtue, but through nature. If there is sin in them it could never be, even in the faintest degree, sensual sin. Of such life we human beings have absolutely no experience, yet it is one of the very first conclusions we must admit when we state that angels are spirits. Attractive as the notion of angels has become to Christian imagination, there is no softness, no sentimentality in true Catholic angelology.

6. *In the sphere of nature an angel cannot err, either in intellect or will.*

This may sound astonishing to our ears, for we hear much of the instability of all created things; yet it follows directly upon the simplicity of spirit-nature. There cannot be in an angel any source of sin or error within his own sphere of existence, but he may sin and err in the mysteries of grace, as those mysteries are above him. Here again I must refer the reader to the chapters on Angelic Sanctity and Spirit Sin.

7. *An angel never goes back on a decision once taken.*

There ought to be little difficulty in our admitting such a trait in the mentality of a spirit, for we admire such a characteristic even in man. There is this difference between obstinacy and strength of resolve in man—that obstinacy comes from narrowness of view, while strength of resolve comes truly from a wide grasp of a fact, of its circumstances, and its implications. The perspicacious man need not alter his views and decisions, because he has seen so clearly the true issues of a thing from the very beginning. Vacillation of purpose in man comes from a predominance of the sentimental element over the intellectual element.

With spirits, as may easily be perceived, there could be no such source of weakness, no such hesitancy of purpose. At a glance they perceive a truth, either theoretical or practical; they see all its aspects, all its consequences, and there are no lower powers in them that could act under impressions of a more mobile kind, and deflect their clear reason and their entirely spiritual will from its first course.

8. *The angelic mind starts with fullness of knowledge, and it is not, like the human mind, subject to gradual development.*

In this we have the profoundest difference between spirit intellect and human intellect. A spirit starts his existence fully endowed with all knowledge; he is never a learner in the true sense of the word, as man is a learner. It may be said of an angel that he applies his knowledge to new objects, but he does not acquire ideas that were not infused into him by the Creator in the very making of him.

9. *An angel may directly influence another created intellect, but he cannot act directly on another created will.*

The former part of this theorem seems, at first sight, to contradict the last theorem, which said that angels never learn in the real sense of the word. Yet much of Catholic theology is taken up with the mutual illuminations of the angels—that one angelic mind illumines another angelic mind. The contradiction is merely apparent. Such influence as the theological term of illumination implies is not the teaching of the ignorant, but a communication of messages from higher spheres of divine commands for which the angelic mind is prepared, and to which it is attuned. Speaking colloquially, we may say that no angelic mind is ever taken by surprise by any communication that reaches it from the council chamber of God. Spirits, then, may act on each other's minds, but it is a sacrosanct principle with Catholic theology that God alone has power to act directly upon a created will. A creature may entice, may persuade, may tempt the will, but it can never touch it directly.

10. *Angels have free will; they are capable of love and hatred.*

Freedom of will is the very essence of ethical perfection, and angels have always been supposed to be ethically good. Love and hatred must be taken in their case, not in the sense of a passion, of a sentiment, but as representing either affinities or oppositions of a will which knows of no sensual attachments.

11. *Angels know material things and individual things.*

12. *Angels do not know the future; they do not know the secret thoughts of other rational creatures; they do not know the mysteries of grace, unless such things be freely revealed to them, either by God or by the other rational creatures.*

Our eleventh and twelfth theorems are clear by their very enunciation. Angelic knowledge is not only of abstract things, but of concrete things. The future free acts of created rational beings are not knowable to a created intellect. God alone contemplates them with infallible security of vision in the light of his eternity. For the same reasons which make it impossible for a spirit to act directly on the will of any rational creature, we say that the secret thoughts of the heart of man or the mind of a spirit are hidden, unless freely revealed by the one who thinks the thought.

In every thought there is an act of will, because I think when I will and I think what I will, but the hiddenness of the will covers my very thoughts. The mysteries of grace are the decision, not of a created will, but of the will of God. A fortiori it will ever be far beyond a created spirit's ken to find out what God is thinking, unless God be pleased to reveal his thoughts.

IV

Angelic Multitude and Hierarchy

The idea of multitude has always been associated with heavenly spirits. Though in our Scriptures they are never shown in multitudes in the execution of work, they are always many when they are shown in as praising God or as forming his Court:

> And suddenly there was with the angel a multitude of the heavenly army praising God, and saying: Glory to God in the highest: and on earth peace to men of good will (Luke 2:13-14).

One angel is seen delivering the message of Christ's Nativity to the shepherds, but a multitude of spirits is heard to sing the praises of God. In the Book of Daniel isolated spirits are sent forth with great power, but when the Ancient of Days is seen by the prophet sitting on his throne there is again multitude in the spirit world:

> Thousands and thousands ministered to him, and ten thousand times a hundred thousand stood before him (Dan 7:10).

Thus too, in the Apocalypse, four angels are seen, "standing on the four corners of the earth and holding the four winds of the earth, that they should not blow upon the earth nor upon the sea nor upon any tree" (Rev 7:1); but there is "heard the voice of many angels round about the throne, and the living creatures and the ancients (and the number of them was thousands of thousands)" (Rev 7:2).

Again in the Apocalypse we see judgment being executed on earth by seven angels, of whom each one holds a vial full on the anger of God, and successively, not simultaneously, they each pour our their vial upon the earth; but when Christ comes forth in triumph he is surrounded by the armies that are in heaven:

> And he was clothed with a garment sprinkled with blood, and his name is called the Word of God. And the armies that are in heaven followed him on white horses, clothed in fine linen, white and clean (Rev 19:13-14).

From this we may gather that in Scriptural thought spirit multitude has a special significance—we might call it the notion of society; that the heavenly spirits are God's society, and that multitude refers not so much to the variety of external missions as to the variety of contemplation of God in himself. In other words, the concept of multitude in spirits is something very different from the concept of multitude in material things.

Number is indeed a marvel of material nature; even the human race has that astonishing factor of number: God has multiplied the children of men. St. Thomas remarks wisely that with material things, man not excluded, number supplements the weakness of the species; a species is saved from death, from disappearance, through its numbers, and the weaker the species the greater its numbers.

It is evident that when we come into the spirit world the notion of number must take a different form, and when we say that angels are innumerable we mean something quite other than the idea suggested if we say, for instance, that the pebbles on the shore are innumerable. In material things number is rather a necessity than a perfection, in spiritual things multitude means perfection, and cannot mean anything else.

This point of theology is approached most satisfactorily if we bear in mind what I have insinuated already—that in our Scriptures spirit-multitude is always associated with the society of God, with the praise and contemplation of his perfection. Spirits are multiplied for this very end, that the perfections of God may be reflected more and more completely. If we take this as the starting-point we shall readily see the beauty of traditional Catholic doctrine which holds that spirits exceed in number anything that we know. The whole idea of multitude is changed; one angel reflects God's glory in one way, another angel in another way, and multitude is something very perfect for this precise reason that it is the image of a perfection which is absolutely inexhaustible.

Such ideas are not connected with the numberless in the material world. We do not find any special beauty in the "innumerable" of the physical world, but the "in-

numerable" of the spirit world are expressions of beauty
ever more and more complete. So we find startling theories held by our theologians—theories which sometimes
do not approve themselves to thinkers whose intellect is
more the servant of imagination than they would themselves admit.

St. Thomas makes it one of the cornerstones of his
angelology that there are no two angels of the same species; that there are no two angels equal in nature; that the
angelic world constitutes an ever-ascending progression
of spiritual substances, each one higher than the other.
With this he maintains the traditional view that spirits
are innumerable, holding a principle which makes such
a view quite acceptable; that it is the proper mission of
the spirits to reflect, in a created fashion, divine perfection; that every spirit does so in his own way; and that an
infinite ascending hierarchy of spirits cannot exhaust the
wealth of God's reflected beauty.

Number has become something very different in such
philosophy from what it is in the calculations of the phys-
icist and the naturalist. It is a thing of dignity, not a mere
juxtaposition of beings side by side. There are, I admit,
a good many theologians to whom this view seems too
bold; they would more willingly talk of brother angels,
of many spirits of the same rank, glorified and spiritual-
ized human beings, in fact, which constitute a heavenly
nation. But I think a very little consideration will show
that imagination plays a large part in the opposition to
the great Thomistic angelology; the angelic crowds of a

Fra Angelico are certainly crowds of brother angels, not hierarchies of spirits.

I ought to say that St. Thomas has deduced his theory of essential variation between angel and angel from the profounder principle of spirit nature. As angels are not united with bodily frames, the great metaphysician finds it impossible to distinguish between spirit and spirit, except on the grounds that they all differ as one species differs from another species. Put quite simply, the idea comes to this: that there are no two angels alike, nor any two angels of equal rank. This view is certainly very commendable from the metaphysical point of view, and, though it may in a way bewilder the imagination, it contributes towards a clearer understanding of what is meant by angelic multitude. It is not an endless repetition within the same plane of being, as is the case even with man; it is, on the contrary, an ever fresh addition to the permanent and essential beauties of the universe.

These considerations lead us on naturally to the treatment of hierarchy among angels. It is one of the best-established doctrines of Christian angelology that there is a diversity of hierarchic gradation among the heavenly spirits. Our Scriptures tell us the names of nine different angelic orders, usually classified in the following succession, beginning with the lowest hierarchy: Angels, Archangels, Principalities, Powers, Virtues, Dominations, Thrones, Cherubim, and Seraphim. These nine choirs are again distinguished into three orders, the impression having prevailed in Christian tradition that there is a certain community of nature, genius, and mission in these triple sets of spiritual categories. That kinship is usually expressed in three different affinities: Seraphim, Cherubim, and Thrones are associated together; then Dominations, Virtues, and Powers; finally Principalities, Archangels, and Angels.

The first question one asks is this: is this ninefold hierarchy exhaustive, so that it may be said to describe the whole angelic world? We cannot speak with certainty, yet it would seem that with the Cherubim and Seraphim we have reached the limits of the spirit world, for these sublime beings are constantly spoken of as the nearest unto God of the whole mighty creation. But no doubt this query is answered more completely if we can give a satisfactory explanation of angelic hierarchy itself. Certainly no theologian need admit that an angelic choir, say the choir of angels, is constituted of spirit beings of the same rank. A moment ago I said that some of the best theology holds that equality of rank is not possible amongst spirits, as each one is a hierarchy in the ever-ascending scale of beings; we must, then, give to angelic hierarchies and orders a very wide meaning, nay, an indefinite meaning, and it would be again indulging our imagination if we made of those nine choirs nine different classes of spirits.

The secrets which are revealed to us in those traditional names are just the few hints given to us of the glorious variety in God's spiritual world. To make of those names categories and exclusive partitions would be contrary to the intentions of the Spirit who whispered the great secrets. We are expected to multiply, not to divide, in our thoughts of the heavenly citizens. We should not divide them into classes, but we should be ready for endless varieties of spiritual splendors.

Hierarchy in the angelic world is not primarily a matter of grace, but a matter of nature. If angels differ in grace it is because they differ in nature, grace being granted to them according to the capacity of their nature; such seems to be the more probable theological view. St. Thomas is quite liberal in his treatment of the meaning of hierarchy and of the angelic orders within that hierarchy. He says that within the nine choirs we make three divisions "on account of our imperfect knowledge," *propter confusam notitiam*, because we do not know more than the vaguest outline of their functions; but did we know more clearly, then we should really see that every angel is in himself an order, because he fulfills a mission in himself, complete and not interchangeable:

> If we knew perfectly the offices of the angels and their differences, then we should know that every angel has his proper office and his proper order in the universe, and this much more than any star, though it be hidden from us. (*Summa*, I, q. 108, a. 3).

We have only the vaguest hints as to the Specific functions covered by those great names of Seraph, Cherub, Thrones, etc. In so free a matter, doctors are allowed to differ. As a sample of the speculations to which those holy names have given rise we may quote St. Thomas who, in his turn, cites the words of the pseudo-Dionysius:

> Let us then first examine the reason for the ordering of
> Dionysius, in which we see that ... the highest hierarchy
> contemplates the ideas of things in God himself; the second
> in the universal causes; and the third in their application
> to particular effects. And because God is the end not only
> of the angelic ministrations, but also of the whole creation,
> it belongs to the first hierarchy to consider the end; to the
> middle one belongs the universal disposition of what is to
> be done; and to the last belongs the application of this dis-
> position to the effect, which is the carrying out of the work;
> for it is clear that these three things exist in every kind of
> operation. So Dionysius, considering the properties of the
> orders as derived from their names, places in the first hier-
> archy those orders the names of which are taken from their
> relation to God, the Seraphim, Cherubim, and Thrones; and
> he places in the middle hierarchy those orders whose names
> denote a certain kind of common government or disposi-
> tion, the Dominations, Virtues, and Powers; and he places
> in the third hierarchy the orders whose names denote the
> execution of the work, the Principalities, Angels, and Arch-
> angels (I, q. 108, a. 6).

Though it be commonly admitted, as we shall see in
another chapter, that the lower order of spirits, called, with
a more constant appropriation of language, the angels, are
those spirits who watch over man, in fact, the guardian
angels, we need not therefore hold that they are spirits of
the same rank; they differ essentially amongst themselves
and there is only one spirit who may be truly called the
lowest spirit. The guardianship of man by the angels is not

so much a matter of the personal dignity of the spirit as a matter of the influence he is pleased to exert on man.

To an objector who would like all spirits, at least those within the same hierarchy, to be equal, on the ground that all men have an angel guardian, and that it would not be suitable that the guardians of beings so similar as men should themselves differ essentially, St. Thomas answers that it is not truly a question of angelic essence so much as of angelic power. The results of that power are similar whatever the greatness of the spirit that exerts it.

It might be said that in many of the angelophanies narrated in our Scriptures the multitude of angels need not have been more than an impression on mortal minds of multitude when there was in reality no multitude. There is, however, an insistence on the number of spirits in the Bible narrative which it would be temerarious to represent invariably as merely a subjective impression on the minds of those men who saw the angels. There are, moreover, passages in the Scriptures which cannot be read otherwise than as meaning truly objective numerousness in the spirit world. Thus in the Epistle to the Hebrews the company of many thousands of angels is stated to be one of the elements of the Christian election:

> You are come to Mount Sion, and to the city of the living God, the heavenly Ierusalem, and to the company of many thousands of angels (Heb. 22:22).

V

The Guardian Angels

It is a favorite theme with St. Thomas Aquinas to represent the whole physical world as being entrusted by God to the keeping of the angels. The stars in their courses are watched by the mighty spirits; nations are committed to the care of a heavenly prince, and there is no part of the universe which does not feel the breath of those whose mind beholds the countenance of God.

An all-pervading principle governs the theology of the spirit ministry—namely, an inferior thing in creation is invariably under the tutelage of a higher thing. To this great law there is no exception. The universe is held together with the golden threads of spirit bower as well as with the coarser sinews of natural energy. As a principle in its vast and indeterminate form this doctrine is very beautiful, and we should not go beyond this generic outline of a great truth; we cannot fill it up with specific facts and details, for the very reason that spirit power, however and wherever exerted, could not be observable in the physical order, precisely because it transcends the physical order.

One objection against this comprehensive theory of theology ought not to be made, that under such an hypothesis physical laws would become superfluous, as spirit activity and will would be the ruling elements of the universe. The theological theory of the universe leaves the physical theory completely untouched. It supposes, however, that there is in the physical universe a tendency to decay and a danger of disorder, however remote, however transcending observable phenomena, which is constantly being corrected by influences of a higher order. Nor ought we to consider those created activities of the spirits superfluous on account of God's omnipresent vigilance over his universe. God multiplies created power, not because he could not effect the result himself, but because it is a more beautiful universe which has a hierarchy of potentialities.

The last form, the ultimate application of that great principle is embodied in the sweet and popular doctrine of the guardian angels. Every human being is under the tutelage of a heavenly spirit, and this in virtue of a natural law. It is not at baptism, it is at birth that every child of Adam is handed over to the keeping of an angel. Great as is the Christian faith in the privileged state of those that are baptized in Christ, it never made the guardianship of the angel an exclusive privilege of the regenerate, but the unbaptized infant shares this divine provision with the baptized. Spirit guardianship of the human race belongs to nature itself. It is true that in the Gospels the angels of the children spoken of are the angels of children who have faith in Christ: "Their angels behold the face of my Father who is in heaven" (Matt 18:10), but Christian tradition has always been emphatic in admitting the universal guardianship of all men, because all men are, at least potentially, the children of God.

The question will be asked at once whether each human being has a separate angel, individually distinct from every other angel. To such a query it would be quite impossible to give an answer, unless we had some authoritative teaching. The work itself of guarding man could not be such as to necessitate the presence of a separate spirit for every separate human being. One angel has power enough to watch over millions with undivided carefulness; but the burden of opinion is in favor of individual angelic guardianship, not of collective protection. But for this we could give no other reason than that the will of God so ordered it.

The protection of spirits must be conceived on entirely spiritual lines. No good purpose is served by false sentiment in a matter so holy. We could not say, with any vestige of truth, that the angel leaves his beautiful heaven for this dreary earth, to take charge of weaklings such as we are; for there is no real departure from the glories of angelic life when a spirit assumes the tutelage of a lower being; more truly the lower being enters into the sphere of activity of one special spirit, just as a planet is kept within the orbit of one special sun.

As I have said already, the angelic guardianship of man by angels is only the last instance of the mighty tutelage of the spirit world over the material world, with this difference, however, that free will comes into play where man is concerned. Here again we must not ask for precise facts, but must be satisfied with the general principle. We must start with the assumption that the human race has fared as it has fared up to now precisely because it has been under the tutelage of spirits—a tutelage which is constant, all-pervading, the most permanent element in the preservation of the human race. We might say, to make this point quite clear, that if the human race had not possessed the spirit tutelage its history would have been very different from what it has been; it would have been infinitely more dismal, though we cannot indicate the facts and events directly attributable to the spirits that watch over man. And what is said of the race is true of every individual human being; we must simply say that this life is what it is because he has been given at his birth into the keeping of an angel.

Very few occasions in a man's mortal career can be traced to the immediate activity of his watching spirit; in fact, unless we are given a special revelation on the subject, not one event in life can be said with certainty to be the direct arrangement of the guardian angel. But we have much more: we have the assurance from our faith that we are being guarded; we have never known any other kind of existence; we might almost say we do not know what it is to be without an angel, just as we do not know what it is to be without the laws of gravity. There is this *a priori* certainty that if individual men are thus entrusted by the Creator to a mighty spirit their whole life is profoundly modified, whether they know it or not.

It would be a mistake to think that the guardianship of the heavenly spirits is given to man only as the result of prayer; it is given absolutely, as a final, unalterable dispensation of God's providence. This spiritual tutelage is meant above all things to keep the human race and human individuals in perfection of nature, and we may say without any exaggeration that the human race would have succumbed long ago to enemies, to deleterious influences, but for the ever-correcting, ever-defending intervention of those benign powers.

Prayer to the angels is, of course, an act of piety much to be commended and most fruitful, for it is in our power to make use of that great tutelage to an extent which varies greatly according to each man's good will; just as prayer to God, in another sphere, makes the divine Majesty more and more propitious, though it could not be said that God would have no thought of man unless man prayed. There is a providence on the part of God which is absolute and independent of man's good will. In the same sense there is a spiritual tutelage of the human race and of every individual being which transcends the vacillation of man's ethical state; the race is kept from destruction and internal dissolution for God's own purposes, we might almost say, in spite of itself.

The sins of men are no signs that men are not guarded by good spirits, for, as St. Thomas says so well, we can act against the good instigations of the spirit that is outside us as we can act against the good instincts that are within us (I, q. 113, a. 1, ad 3). The good instincts remain as a great reality in spite of our prevarication; so likewise the angelic inspiration remains in spite of our voluntary deafness to it. Nor could it be said that the spirits work in vain, even with those who are lost. Not only are we to suppose, again with St. Thomas, that the most perverted of men are kept from greater evils by their heavenly guardians, but the evil committed by one man is kept in check by those spirits of sanctity, lest it work havoc in other men (I, q. 113, a. 4, ad 3).

This angelic guardianship is something natural, something normal, as normal as the great powers of the physical cosmos. The spirits have not received a mission to interfere with man's free action; they have received a mission to save man from the results of his own evil deeds as far as is compatible with the higher dictates of God's justice. When an angel shows his protecting power manifestly, as when he delivered Peter from the prison, you have a miraculous intervention which ought not to be taken as the criterion of the ordinary working of spirit tutelage. There can be miracles of angelic intervention, as there can be miracles of divine intervention; but they are exceptions; God and his angels work unceasingly for man's welfare.

Illumination of man's mind is the most direct and most constant effect of the angelic tutelage; according to St. Thomas, it is not too much to say that the human race is kept in mental equilibrium through the unceasing watchfulness of the good spirits (I, q. 113, a. 5, ad 2). There is, in spite of individual aberrations, a sanity of thought in mankind which makes all men to agree on some universal principles. Would it not be a beautiful thing to consider such unanimity as the result of the supervision of the spirits? Certainly Catholic theology would not be loth to encourage such a view.

Then there is that extremely important office of the protecting angels to ward off the darkening influence of evil spirits. So far we have been assuming that spirits are good, but Christian revelation does not allow such optimism to be complete; there are bad spirits just as there are good spirits, as we shall see in one of the following chapters. An immense amount of angelic work for man's benefit must be of the defensive kind; man could never know, unless it were revealed to him, from what evils he has been saved. The spirits fight for us to a great extent without our knowledge, their mission is essentially one of guardianship of a lower being, and it is carried out quite independently of that lower being's participation or recognition. It is truly a trust, and the spirit is responsible for the full discharge of that trust to the heavenly Father by whom it was committed to him.

So far we have considered angelic guardianship in the life of nature, as one only of the great forces that keep the universe together; but it is evident that we cannot separate man's higher and supernatural destiny from his natural life; we are called to the kingdom of heaven, the angels see in us their fellow-participants in the graces of the Holy Ghost, and they have the additional mission of leading us to heaven.

In connection with this supernatural purpose of the spirit tutelage, St. Thomas makes a few wise remarks which, in a way, justify the common Catholic opinion that each man is under the protection of a separate spirit, that there is no disproportion between the ward and the guardian. Man's destiny being eternal happiness, it is not too much that it should be watched over by one whose nature is unchangeably great. Again, the secrets of grace are the greatest secrets, they are God's personal province, they are the dealings of the adorable Trinity, not *en masse*, but with individual rational creatures; only God knows the graces that make up the predestination of the elect.

It is not astonishing, therefore, St. Thomas would say, that individual angels are chosen to watch over human souls which are treated with such preference by God himself. God has messages to communicate to an angel about a definite human being, which are truly the secrets of the divine counsel:

> Are they not all ministering spirits sent to minister for them who shall receive the inheritance of salvation (Heb 1:14)?

St. Thomas has a good commentary on these words:

> If we think of the last result of the spirit tutelage, which is the receiving of the inheritance, the angelic ministry is effective only in the case of those who receive the inheritance. Nevertheless, it is to be maintained that the ministry of the

angels is not denied to other men, although in their case the ministry falls short of its final result, the leading on to salvation. Yet in their case also the ministry of the angels is not without its efficacies as they are kept from many evils (I, q. 113, a. 5, ad 1).

VI

ANGELIC SANCTITY

Not once in the Scriptures, so full of angelic incidents, do we discover a vestige of moral imperfection in an angel, nor do we ever find that one is rebuked for anything that he does. The angels are perfect in all their ways. Angelic sanctity is, for us Christians, a self-evident fact. Our theology greatly helps our spiritual intuition, and starting from certain clearly proven principles it has uttered beautiful things on the purity of the angels and the eminence of their holiness. What we know concerning the nature of a spirit and what we know about grace stands us in good stead when we come to look at the lives of our heavenly brothers. As spirits they can never do anything by halves, they cannot be imperfect, they cannot act remissly, the whole energy of their intellect and will is given to every one of their movements in the ethical order—if one may speak of ethics in connection with spirits. Venial sin is quite unthinkable in angelic morality; it is easier for us to understand a total collapse of the angelic will than a partial deflection; a spirit may choose a wrong end, but he could not choose it with less than the whole impetuosity of his nature.

Bearing in mind the excellency of a spirit nature, our best theologians have said that, in its natural sphere, on its own plane, so to speak, a purely spiritual being cannot fail either in mind or in will, but it could fail with regard to things that are above it; in other words, with regard to the supernatural. This point we shall elaborate more completely when we come to speak of angelic sin; for the present let us feel happy in the thought that the angels have not in themselves any weakness, any temptation, any of that division between higher and lower motives which is found in us. They have not the conflicts of any kind of concupiscence, they have no doubts, they are not in danger of forming precipitate judgements; and all this in virtue of the very principles of their nature.

But it is a matter of Catholic faith that the spirits have been raised to the supernatural order, that they received grace, and that they possess sanctifying grace and the gifts of the Holy Ghost, just like the Christian man here on earth. There is not in them the division between flesh and spirit, between a higher and a lower nature, but there is in them the division between the natural and the supernatural. They have been raised above themselves for a destiny greater than the spirit destiny; they are meant to behold God face to face in Beatific Vision—an end so lofty that no spirit, however excellent, is capable of it without a gratuitous infusion of those higher qualities called grace. Grace with the angels, then, could not be a medicine to heal the wounds of a fall, as it is with man to so large an extent, nor could it be a help to powers weak and anemic in themselves—spirits have no wounds, spirits are never weak—but grace with angels is essentially the lifting up of a perfect being to a still higher plane, the initiation of a created mind into the secrets of the Uncreated Mind; and without grace even the supreme spirit would be incapable of that communion with God which constitutes the life of charity with the Father, the Son, and the Holy Ghost.

So we have to assume at once that, with regard to the final and supernatural union with God, the spirits are in the same position as man. It may be said that spirits, both discarnate and incarnate, are equidistant from the final goal of Beatific Vision, and that the angels, equally with us, are in need of the grace of God to reach communion with him. There is, therefore, at once brought about, through the supernatural, a true community of condition between man and the spirits. Abysmal as may be the differences of minds and wills between man and spirit, and between the spirits themselves, the differences disappear, are as nothing, in presence of that true infinitude—the Vision of God. Just as in astronomy there are no real differences when distances are said to be infinite; the surface of our earth may appear extremely uneven to us who dwell upon it, there are the high mountains and the deep ravines, but looked at from the fixed stars such unevenness is as if non-existent.

Though there is a radical difference between the natural and the supernatural even in the spirits, it is the more common opinion that all spirits were created with the gift of grace in them already; this would only mean that between the production of nature and the infusion of grace there was no time interval, but there is always the profound and essential differentiation between the two elements, nature and grace. The spirits were not created in the clear Vision of God; this was to be the goal towards which they had to aim, the reward of their fidelity; they were created in grace outside the Vision of God, with the invitation to rise up to that supreme Vision; they were created, says St. Thomas, not in the heaven of the Trinity, but in the empyrean heaven; from the one they were expected to ascend to the other. The *caelum sanctae Trinitatis*, "heaven of the Holy Trinity" (I, q. 56, a. 4, ad 3), is the heaven of the clear Vision of God face to face. The angels did not find themselves in that heaven to begin with; they found themselves in that other heaven which may be called the supremest place of the natural cosmos, whilst the heaven of the Vision is that glorious kingdom which has been prepared specifically for the elect from the beginning of the world:

> Then shall the king say to them on his right hand: Come, ye blessed of my Father, possess you the kingdom prepared for you from the foundation of the world (Matt 25:34).

We say that the angels merited eternal life as truly as man merits eternal life, through correspondence with that supernatural grace that was in them, for the spirits as well as man had their day of trial, they were wayfarers between their earth and their heaven, between the *caelum empyreum*, "Empyrean Heaven," and the *caelum sanctae Trinitatis*. These principles are certain. How long did their trial last? Here we must leave imagination alone. Let us take it for granted that whatever element of duration there was in the angelic wayfaring it amounted in worth and spirit intensity to the value of the longest human life. Theologians would say that the first act of the angels was self-consciousness, the second act a full cooperation with the grace that was in them, and the third act the clear Vision or, shall we say, the flight from the *caelum empyreum* to the *caelum sanctae Trinitatis*. Only let us remember that centuries of human activity would pale before the energy of that single act of the spirits between creation and glorification.

We have already spoken of the profound inequalities of the angelic natures; we said that they were an ever-ascending hierarchy of spiritual substances. The question arises, then, whether grace and the supernatural endowment were meted out to them according to the capacity of their natures, so that an angel of a higher grade in nature is also of a higher grade in grace and of a higher grade in glory. This we may readily grant: a Cherub is greater than an inferior spirit in all his endowments, both natural and supernatural. Human beings are all of the same nature, but they receive grace in a variety of measures; some are given one talent, some five. We may say that with man nature is not the measure of grace; let us ever bear in mind that one human being, Mary, the Mother of God, has received grace more abundantly than any other creature.

With the spirits, however, there seems to be a fitness that grace should exactly follow the perfection of nature. Men, though of one nature, work with various intensities; spirits, on the contrary, work at all times to the full extent of their energies, there can be no intermittencies, no relaxations, there can be no progress—in the human sense of the word—so it seems the wiser thing in theology to concede to the vaster mind and the vaster will an ampler manifestation of the counsels of God's supernatural order.

After these exact theorizings on angelic sanctity we could give our imagination free scope and let it enjoy the spectacle of that inexpressibly great holiness, but whatever we could imagine would fall short of the reality.

The vision of Isaiah is the greatest imaginative presentment of angelic sanctity:

> In the year that King Uzziah died, I saw the Lord sitting upon a throne high and elevated: and his train filled the temple. Upon it stood the seraphims: the one had six wings, and the other had six wings: with two they covered his face, and with two they covered his feet, and with two they flew. And they cried one to another, and said: Holy, Holy, Holy, the Lord God of Hosts, all the earth is full of his glory. And the lintels of the doors were moved at the voice of him that cried: and the house was filled with smoke. And I said: Woe is me, because I have held my peace; because I am a man of unclean lips, and I dwell in the midst of a people that hath unclean lips, and I have seen with my eyes the King the Lord

of hosts. And one of the seraphim flew to me: and in his hand was a live coal, which he had taken with the tongs off the altar. And he touched my mouth, and said: Behold this hath touched thy lips, and thy iniquities shall be taken away, and thy sin shall be cleansed. And I heard the voice of the Lord, saying: Whom shall I send, and who shall go for us? And I said: Lo, here am I. Send me (Isa 6:1-8).

There is, however, one aspect of angelic sanctity which we might almost call its moral side: it is expressed generally as the obedience of the angels—more truly it might be called their "order"; that the spirits keep the order in which they are created, carry out the missions which are entrusted to them, that all their mighty activities are an unceasing dependence on God's will; above all, that they accept the kingship of a nature lower than their own. They have not rebelled against the exaltation of the human nature in Christ Jesus, and the Catholic Church never ceases to speak of the Mother of God as Queen of the angels. This observance of the order established by God is the true angelic virtue, the one thing in which they might fail; it might even be called their temptation, and if the temptation be overcome, it is their victory.

That there was some such victory is evident from more than one passage in the Scriptures; angels are considered as having come out of some great spiritual war triumphant in the moral order:

And there was a great battle in heaven: Michael and his angels fought with the dragon, and the dragon fought, and his angels. And they prevailed not: neither was their place found any more in heaven. And that great dragon was cast out, that old serpent, who is called the devil and Satan, who seduceth the whole world. And he was cast unto the earth: and his angels were thrown down with him (Rev 12:7-9).

Fidelity to God over a great, a mightily debated issue seems to be an essential portion of angelic sanctity.

VII

Spirit Sin

When Christ speaks of the reward of the elect he represents it in the form of an invitation to take possession of the kingdom that had been "prepared from the foundation of the world (Matt 25:34). The chastisement of the wicked he speaks of as "everlasting fire prepared for the devil and his angels" (Matt 25:41). This terrible penal arrangement is not said to be, like the gracious provision for merit, *a constitutione mundi*, "from the foundation of the world." Satan and his followers were not created evil; there was no thought in God's first providence of an *ignis aeternus*, "eternal fire." No Christian doubts the existence of evil powers in the spirit world, but no Christian considers those evil powers to be anything but a miscarriage, through the creature's act, of the Creator's first plan. There is no evil principle having, so to speak, an estate by itself; all evil is an apostasy of a being that was primarily good; all evil is a bad use of the good things of God.

It is an extremely difficult point of theology to explain sin in connection with spirits. If our Scriptures were not so full of the activities of evil spirits the temptation might arise to regard all wickedness as a human phenomenon. The sinfulness of man is a thing of daily experience; we can explain it through man's composite nature, through man's passions and difficulties; man is morally a sinner, as socially he is a savage; both sin and barbarity are patient of explanation. But how shall we arrive at any satisfactory explanation of spirit lapses?

If we regarded spirits only as more agile forms of human beings, then we might give them passions and instincts whose workings, sooner or later, would entangle them in difficult positions. But spirits are perfect, at any rate those spirits in which Catholic theology believes; it is their very essence to be perfect in nature; we cannot think of any sort of allurement which might deflect them from their path.

We might, as a first attempt at explanation, give this reason for a possible lapse in the spirit world: that spirits, since they are created beings, are finite beings, and that no finite being can claim absolute immunity from every possible error of mind, or will. In this universality the principle may be considered as the remote cause of sin in all but God himself; yet this does not work in Catholic theology as a cause of the fall of the angels, except as a most vague explanation. A spirit has no ignorances, has no weakness of mind; his nature is so perfect that there is nothing for which he can wish or to which he can aspire; though he is finite, he is complete in his sphere.

With great wisdom St. Thomas has discarded every sort of motive for the angelic lapse that is not entirely spiritual, that savors more of imagination than of intelligence. He teaches with steady persistence that no spirit in his natural sphere can transgress or err in any way. But if the spirit be taken, so to speak, out of his natural order and placed in another, a higher order—the supernatural order—then there is the possibility of a refusal; the spirit may refuse to accept or to hold something that is above his order; he may, in fact, rebel against the order of God. This is the only tenable theological explanation of the fall of the angels, and I must develop it more amply.

Through the supernatural a spirit is taken out of his sphere into a higher one; but this higher sphere means essentially a community of life with all other spirits thus favored; it means community with lower spirits; it means community with man himself. The higher grace is indeed the more excellent gift, but it is also the more universal gift. The natural greatness of the angel is a glory which has no equal; it is a singular perfection which is without a rival. A spirit may thus choose to enter into communion with the supernatural or to remain entirely in his own sphere, preferring his own natural excellency to the communion of the universal family of God.

St. Thomas says that some spirits chose the second alternative; they preferred their natural glory in its isolation to the community of the supernatural charity; and this is the fall of the angels. It is pride—because they elected excellency without reference to the more excellent good; it is rebellion—because the Will of God was that they should accept the supernatural; it is envy—not in the sense of the dark human passion, but in the sense of an opposition to a holy thing, the grace of God.

All other sins must be taken more or less metaphorically in the case of the fallen angels. When it is said that Satan desired to be like unto God we could not take it as a reasonable view that he aspired to be as great as the divine Creator; no spirit could be capable of such folly; but as St. Thomas puts it:

> In this wise did Satan wish unlawfully to be like unto God, because he desired as the final goal of happiness that which was within the power of his own nature, turning away his desires from the supernatural happiness which is obtained through the grace of God. Or it might be said also that if he desired as his last end that resemblance with God which comes from grace, he wanted to possess it through the power of his nature, not through the divine help according to God's order (I, q. 63, a. 3).

All this is very clear in a way; it is opposition to the supernatural order which constitutes the *malitia angelica*, it is "spirit rebellion." It is said sometimes that the mystery of the Incarnation was revealed to the spirits, and that their unwillingness to adore the God-Man was their fall. This would only be another expression of the same doctrine that angels fell through a deliberate opposition to the supernatural, as the Incarnation is the highest phase of the supernatural.

So we may leave this matter in that wise moderation in which it was left by St. Thomas:

> In this way did the angel sin, because he turned his free will to his own good without reference to the (higher) rule of the divine Will (I, q. 63, a. 1, ad 4).

The great theologian thinks that such a sin is compatible with complete knowledge of means and end, principles and results, and that such a sin can be found in a being devoid at his creation of all perverse inclination and of all passion. It is essentially a free election of a definite state, and it is an irrevocable election.

All other perversities which are attributed to Satan come from this free election, for it is not a passive state of personal excellency which Satan has chosen, it is of necessity an active opposition to the higher order. Thus every other sin is truthfully predicated of the evil spirits, because with every means in their power do they wage war against the supernatural order; they are the great disturbers of the divine order. Satan always sins, Satan is mendacious, Satan is a murderer; and he incites man to the foulest sins, not because of any pleasure he himself could have in the works of the flesh, but because the works of the flesh render man unfit for the grace of God and exclude him from the supernatural order.

It is quite in keeping with all we have said when we hear the Scriptures stating that it is Satan's chief occupation to deceive man, deceiving him in the most subtle manner and transforming himself into an angel of light.

The difference between natural excellency and supernatural grace may be called a subtle difference, and man's great deception lies in this: that through the splendor of natural gifts he is led to despise the grace of God.

It is a simple consequence of all that has been said to maintain that the evil angels keep all their natural gifts without any diminution; they even keep their order; they remain in the state which they elected, yet they are banished completely from the supernatural order; and as the supernatural order is the one which must ultimately triumph, Satan and his followers are truly cast out into eternal darkness, into the fire which will be their prison for ever. They are darkened in their intellects with regard to the mysteries of grace, with regard to the counsels of God's free will, but not with regard to things which constitute the glories of the natural universe; the knowledge of the natural universe is part of their very being, and they could not lose it without losing their identity.

In the foregoing considerations we have spoken as if the supernatural were offered to the spirits, when some accepted it and some refused. In the preceding chapter we said that the more probable opinion is that all spirits were created in the supernatural, so they were given no option as to its acceptance or its refusal. This, of course, does not alter the worth of the theological opinion. Though the spirits were created in the supernatural, they were free to remain in it or to forsake it, because it was something essentially added unto their spirit-estate, not something inherent in their very being.

The demons are called apostate spirits, because they fell away from the vocation and the grace to which they had been called by the Creator; they did not persevere in their supernatural election as did the good angels. It is obviously a thing self-evident in theology that when once a created spirit has been admitted to the clear Vision of God all falling away becomes impossible. The spirits that lapsed had never attained to that Beatific Vision.

VIII

EVIL SPIRITS AND MAN

It could not be said that the spirit tutelage, of which through a wise dispensation of Providence man is the object, has a direct counterpart in the sad influences of the fallen spirits on the destinies of the human race. We are not in reality standing, as it were, between two spirits, a good one on our right and a bad one on our left; this would be an exaggerated notion of the activities of the reprobate spirits among the children of men. The angelic tutelage is a divine ordinance, directly willed by God; the temptations of the demons are not, of course, a divine ordinance, they belong to what is called the permissive providence of God; he allows them, but he does not order them. With this reservation made, we may go very far in our belief in the reality of demoniac power in the world.

To begin with, we must bear in mind that whatever may be the explanation of the presence of the evil spirits on our planet, such a presence was not originally brought about by the sin of man. The devil tempted man when he was yet in a state of innocence; the evil spirit was on this earth before human sin had ever been committed. Man's sins have strengthened Satan's position in this world, but it could not be said that they have created it. The presence of the Evil One on this earth in the days of man's innocence is an insoluble mystery.

Nothing is expressed more often and more explicitly by the Roman Church in her various exorcisms and blessings than the idea that evil spirits abide in material things, from which they are driven out by the Church's triumphant power of sanctifying and consecrating the visible elements which are the basis of human life. The human body itself may be the dwelling of an evil spirit: this might be called the silent occupation of this earth by Satan, a thing full of mystery and independent in its origin of man's consent to Satan's evil suggestions. But there is also the more manifest presence of these dark beings. It would be temerarious to belittle what the early Fathers said of the power of the demons in the pagan temples, in the idols, in the groves and caverns where heathen rites were performed. The demons were loud in their utterances through the mouth of the idols, and many are the incidents in early Church history which prove that the pagan nations were accustomed to exhibitions of unseen powers which could never be considered as powers of light. Then we have, through all the centuries of the Christian spiritual warfare, most authentic records of manifest activities of the demons. The servants of God are persecuted by fierce powers, visibly, physically, in open daylight, as it were. The best-known case in modern hagiography is the persecution which the holy Curé d'Ars suffered in his body from his spiritual adversaries.

The more recondite temptations of Satan which concern man's religious life hold a middle place between that silent occupation of this earth by Satan, and the tumultuous showing forth of his power in cases of possession or obsession. Satan tempts man to sin, not manifestly but secretly, in such a wise that it is not possible for man to discover whether an evil prompting comes from his own nature or from the suggestion of an alien spirit with a perverted will. Such discernment demands great spiritual gifts, one might even say it requires a special *charisma* which is given only to few. Indeed, it is not necessary for us to know whether an evil propensity is caused by an outside spirit, or is the result of our own evil inheritances; the avoidance of sin is the one thing that matters, and that is always within our power, through God's grace and the assistance of the holy spirits. On the whole, it is more in conformity with Catholic tradition to consider the Christian, with his glorious spiritual armor, as being himself formidable to the devils rather than as living in fear and terror of those beings of darkness.

"Give not place to the devil" (Eph 4:27) is an apostolic precept which reveals the true psychology of diabolical temptations in our spiritual life. Place is given to the devil through any voluntary deflection from the moral order; the evil spirit enters into our life through those weaknesses of which we are guilty through our own carelessness. It is as if infidelity to divine grace could not remain a merely human affair, it has prolongations which man does not intend, but which are unavoidable consequences. We are, in the strong words of one of the Collects, "exposed to the diabolical contagion," *diabolica contagio* (17th Sunday after Pentecost).

The devil's influence on the human masses is no doubt much more powerful than the seduction of individual men, masses are more liable to suggestion, and all we know of mass-psychology makes us fear that, outside the Christian people, Satan's influence on mankind is a very real fact. The devils are, in St. Paul's words, "the rulers of the world of this darkness" (Eph 6:12). I do not mention here that kind of bondage to Satan in which mankind found itself through sin, and from which it has been released through the Cross of Christ, for this aspect of demoniac power belongs rightly to the mystery of Redemption.

Man's intercourse with the demons is a thing which has no counterpart in his relationship with the good spirits. With a good spirit we never hold any intercourse which is not perfectly in the divine order, through the very definition of angelic sanctity. As demons are rebellious spirits, the question may pertinently be put whether it is in the power of man to get into touch with those wicked, but mighty ones, for some selfish end; one would naturally ask: has the devil ever answered man when man has tried to approach him, and to hold intercourse with him? Dark magic has always had a fascination for a certain class of minds, but no doubt most of its claims, if not all of them, belong to the realm of fables. Consulting the devil has always been held to be one of the darkest sins which man can commit.

Spiritism of the modern type is a more serious, a more alarming matter. It does not belong directly to either angelology or demonology, as the modern spiritist claims to hold intercourse with disembodied human spirits; however, there is a strong presumption that spiritistic phenomena, when they are not impostures, are things of evil origin; viewed from that angle, spiritism is only a province of demonology. I am aware, of course, that all modern spiritists repudiate dealings with the dark powers of the unseen world. They claim a purity of intention in their efforts to get into touch with the invisible world, which, no doubt, is sincere in many cases. They say that they want to learn from the spirits the things of the spirits; that they want to come into contact only with the holy ones on the other side. A spiritism thus refined is a most seductive thing, and to refute it, to show its illegality or its immorality, is not possible, to my thinking, apart from revelation, and unless we profess our faith in the guiding authority of the Church. All other arguments against spiritism are based on certain accidental, evil by-products of the practice, or they take for granted the very thing that has to be proved—that spiritism is an intercourse with fallen angels.

We have here a first-rate instance of the beneficent meaning of the guidance of a living Church; it enables us to see clearly, where so many are deceived and led in captivity by the spirit of error who transforms himself into an angel of light. Nothing is sadder than to see the numbers of well-meaning men and women who are held in thralldom by the fascination of contemporary spiritism, for we, as Catholics, know that they have become the playthings of the spirits who have been liars from the beginning.

The circumstance that they are ignorant of the ethical perverseness of the practice does not in the least diminish its evil; they have become the victims of a terrible conspiracy of wickedness in high places, from which we escape unscathed through our loyalty to the guidance of the living Church. As for the Catholic who will not listen to that guidance in these most dangerous matters, I do not see that a merely speculative exposition of the evil of spiritism could possibly have any influence to save him from the worst excesses of unhealthy curiosity.

It may be said that the Catholic Church has her own spiritism, a thing full of health and life; it is her belief that every soul in the state of grace is in spiritual communion with every other soul thus privileged, and that this communion goes beyond mortal life. The Christian here on earth has a most intimate affinity with all elect spirits, angelic and human, in the world to come. The Church holds very definite and very practical views as to the mode in which spirits may approach each other. This profound doctrine is merely a part of the larger truth of the mystical Body of Christ; and we may add that deeper knowledge of the disembodied state into which the spirit of man enters at death will facilitate the intelligence of the Catholic standpoint. Readers may be referred to other portions of Catholic theology for these absorbing matters.

IX

The Society of the Heavenly Citizens

It is evident by all the laws of spiritual life that angelic beings must be, in one way or another, a great element in the constitution of man's eternal happiness. The bliss of the elect will be essentially this—to possess all truth, to be in contact with all reality, to see all beauty. To see the angels, to behold them, must of necessity constitute a source of happiness greater than anything which the visible world could afford; in fact, it is the supreme created source of happiness; God himself, clearly seen in the Beatific Vision, being the uncreated source of happiness. To be with the angels, to see them in their glory, is a most legitimate desire in the heart of man, and the saints of God have often given utterance to such a longing.

We must always keep alive within us that essentially Catholic principle of life, that the possession of the supreme Goodness, God himself, never destroys the appetite for created goodness, but, on the contrary, enhances it;

to see God face to face produces in the minds of the elect a new capacity to see him in his creatures, and where is he seen to greater advantage than in the world of angels, which mirrors back, with an almost infinite power of radiation, the glory of the invisible God?

Moreover, through the communion of supernatural grace man is allied to the angels by the bond of charity, he is not a foreigner but he is a fellow-citizen. There will be this truest exchange of love between man and the heavenly spirits: man, besides beholding the angels in their glory, will hold intercourse with them as citizens of the same kingdom, as the children of the same Father. This intercourse with the heavenly spirits will be the last thing in created love; greater love than that there could not be except man's communion with God himself.

There is, however, something deeper than this association with the angels in vision and love. This association would be possible if the whole human race—I mean the elect human race—remained in its own sphere, on its plane, lower than the angelic world. The human race could be considered as the boundary-line of the whole world of the elect and as its lowest portion. Yet such is not the traditional view of Catholic theology. There is quite a volume of opinion which considers man's association with the angels to be of a more intimate kind, and of a much profounder dispensation. The elect of the human race are believed to be assumed into the very hierarchy of the angels, into the ranks of the Cherubim and Seraphim and all the other orders; the elect of the human race will not be only the outside fringe of the spirit world, they will, on the contrary, be shining stars in every one of the spirit planes.

It is Catholic tradition that the elect of the human race are destined to take the place of the fallen spirits, to fill up the gap made by the apostasies of the rebellious angels. This tradition profoundly modifies man's relationship to the angels; it puts him on a footing of equality with those mighty beings which is the most astonishing of all spiritual exaltations. We could not say with any degree of certainty whether all the elect of the human race are meant to take the place of fallen spirits, but it would seem that no doubt is permissible with regard to God's intention of filling the vacant places in the spirit hierarchies with human beings. God will multiply his graces, and prepare his saints with such power of predestination that not one of the high thrones of spirit life will be found vacant on the day of the consummation of his mighty plan.

That there will be more than mere association of men and angels in the glory of eternity is clear from our Lord's words in speaking of the elect at the resurrection:

> Neither can they die any more: for they are equal to the angels and are the children of God, being the children of the resurrection (Luke 20:36).

This equality means more than a mere similarity, it means a community of privilege which makes of the human elect and the spirit elect one society. This equality is entirely based on grace. Human nature will always remain what it is, vastly inferior to the angelic nature; but such is the power of grace that the inequality of nature is bridged over, and that an elect from the human race may truly become, in all literalness of language, the equal of the highest angel, and that consequently he will be vastly superior to other angels of lower rank.

In this matter, as in most of our philosophizing on spirit-issues, we must be satisfied with the general principle; detail, from the very nature of the case, is not possible to us. Thus we do not know in what proportion the spirits fell or in what proportion they passed into the unchanging glory of the Blessed Vision; we do not know, either, with any degree of certainty, what direction that great cleavage in the heavenly world took when there was that sliding away from God of so many spirits. Did angels of every order fall away? Was there a preponderance of rebellion in any given hierarchy? Did many more fall in the lower than in the higher orders? Such questions cannot be answered with any degree of certainty. St. Thomas is inclined to think that only a minority of the spirits fell away, because, he remarks wisely, to fall away is, in a spirit, against his nature, and things that are contrary to nature happen usually more by way of exception than by way of generality.

It would seem, however, that the supremest spirit fell, and that this mighty prince of light was the cause of the apostasy of many. It is generally considered that Lucifer was that highest spirit who became the Prince of Darkness. We are not concerned here directly with demonology;

our scope is a more consoling one. Whatever height a fallen spirit may have occupied in the scale of being, it is possible for the grace of God to raise man to that height, so that even the throne vacated by Lucifer himself may become the congenital inheritance of some holy human soul.

We need not maintain, of course, as already insinuated, that all human beings who are saved through the grace of Christ are meant to be raised to the angelic hierarchies. Cajetan, the stern theologian of Reformation times, thinks that the children who die and are saved in virtue of baptismal grace, without any personal merit, will remain below the angelic order of election; they will be the true human race in its own setting; they will resemble the angels without being equal to them (*Commentary*, I, q. 108, a.8). Then again there are those human beings who will be absolutely superior by the very laws of their predestination to every angelic order; the blessed Mother of God is certainly one such creature.

The all-pervading principle is this: that grace is greater than nature, greater even than the highest spirit nature, and its scope is vaster than the vastest world. As a confirmation of the doctrine of human substitution for the lost spirits we may quote St. Paul's text:

> Know you not that we shall judge angels? how much more things of this world (1 Cor. 6:3)?

The Apostle evidently alludes to the great judgment at the end of time; judgment will be given to the saints, and they will execute it, not only on this world, but even on the angels—the fallen angels, no doubt. This power of judgment would naturally presuppose, not only equality, but superiority of rank.

In the Western Church virginity is considered to be more particularly the angelic life amongst men, whilst in the Eastern Church the angelic life is more commonly identified with the renouncing of temporal possessions. The striving after higher perfection, after the angelic life in all its aspects, is, in Christian spirituality, a preparation for the higher ranks amongst the angels in the world to come; the martyrs, also, are those who will be found worthy to have their names confessed by the Son of God before the holy angels. Whatever heroism there is amongst Christians in the days of their earthly pilgrimage it gives them a right to a reward which again is fitly expressed by the word "throne."

> To him that shall overcome, I will give to sit with me in my throne: as I also have overcome, and am set down with my Father in his throne (Rev 3:21).

www.ingramcontent.com/pod-product-compliance
Lightning Source LLC
Chambersburg PA
CBHW071907020426
42331CB00010B/2703